KETO
RECIPES

81 Recipes for Quick and Easy
Low-Carb
Step-by-step

By *Luke J. Brown*

TABLE OF CONTENTS

KETO BREAKFAST 6

The Nut Loaf 7
Vegetable-Walnut Pâté 10
Herb-Crusted Tofu 12
Mystical Apple Martini 14
Buttery Almond Blast 16
Cute Bacon Avocado Breakfast Muffins 18
Almond and Vanilla Smoothie 20
Keto Breakfast Cereal with Almond Milk 22
Keto smoked salmon sandwich on spiced pumpkin bread 24
Tuna stuffed avocado 28
Low-carb Vegan Vanilla Protein Shake 30
Low-carb Ginger and Licorice Granola 32
Keto French Toast 33
Keto Green Smoothies 37
Cauliflower Tabouli (Tabbouleh) Salad 38
Breakfast Muffins 39
Matcha Smoothie Bowl 41
Ghee & Coconut Coffee 42
Keto Crème Fruity 43
Yummy Berries with Coconut Cream 44
Old Tale's Bacon Cheddar & Chive Omelet 46
Salad For Early Morning 48
Century Caprese Salad 50
Ham & Mushroom Scramble 51
Mini-ham Quiches 52
Crepes with Nut Butter and Whipped Cream 54
Strawberry-Coconut Porridge 58
Tantalizing Chicken Salad with Bacon 59
Gorgeous Tuna Salad with Avocado 61
Amazing Asian Beef and Coleslaw 62
Shrimp with Sweet and Spicy Chicken 64
Spiced Lime Steak and Asparagus 66
Cheesy-Topped Baked Pork 68
Scrummy Sausage Pie 70

KETO LUNCH 72

- BLACKENED SHRIMP AND ASPARAGUS SKILLET 72
- GARLIC SAUTÉED CABBAGE KALE SKILLET 77
- LOW-CARB VEGAN KEBAB WRAPS WITH GARLIC SAUCE 80
- KETO ZUCCHINI CRAB MELTS 84
- BAGEL OMELET 87
- PORK CHOPS WITH GREEN BEANS AND GARLIC BUTTER 89
- KETO PORK CHOPS WITH BLUE-CHEESE SAUCE 92
- HAM, EGG, AND CHEESE ROLL-UPS 94
- CHICKEN STRIPS & CAULIFLOWER BITES 96
- HOT CURRIED PUMPKIN SOUP 99
- HOT AND SPICY THAI BEEF SALAD 101
- MUSHROOM PIZZA BITES 103
- SESAME CRUSTED TUNA 105
- CHICKEN AND BACON SALAD 107
- BEEF AND CAULIFLOWER SPICY PAN 108
- MEAT LOVER'S STIR FRY 111
- KETO CHICKEN SALAD 114
- KING SIZED CREAMY MUSHROOM WITH CHICKEN 116
- PINNACLE MONTEREY MUG MELT 118
- KETO SMOTHERED CHICKEN 120
- KETO SESAME SALMON 122

KETO DINNER 124

- Keto Pork Chop and Broccoli Casserole 124
- Rotisserie Chicken with Keto Chili Béarnaise Sauce 127
- Easy Shrimp Avocado Salad with Tomatoes 129
- Keto Crispy Bacon with Onion Sauce 135
- Asparagus Soup 137
- Swedish Meatballs 139
- BBQ Chicken Wings with Loaded Mash Cauliflower 141
- Pot Roast 145
- Garlic-Rosemary Pork Chops with Roasted Brussels Sprouts 147
- Chicken Cordon Bleu with Garlic 149
- Keto Bread 149
- Beef Chili 152
- Keto Stuffed Mushrooms 154
- Crazy Grilled Eggplant Panini 156
- Crab-stuffed Mushrooms with Cream Cheese 158
- Coconut Pork Butt Curry 160
- Easy Bacon Prapped Pork Tenderloin 162
- Bacon Net Pork Tenderloin 164
- Sausage, Shrimp and Zucchini Skewers 167

KETO SNACKS AND SWEETS .. 169

- JALAPENO POPPER BALLS 169
- HONEY-KETO MUFFINS 171
- KETO MICROWAVED BROWNIES 173
- CHOCOLATE AD COCONUT CHEESECAKE 175
- CRISPY-BAKED PARSNIP CHIPS 177
- CRISPY-BAKED KALE CHIPS 178
- KETO ENERGY-BOOSTING PROTEIN SHAKE 179

KETO
BREAKFAST

The Nut Loaf

This very popular nut loaf, it's a good way to use any leftover cheese you may have accumulated. The type of cheese you can use is flexible, but try to include some strongly-flavored cheese such as Brie, Gorgonzola, Gruyère, or Smoked Gouda. When making the Almond Pâté, double the recipe so there is some for this nut loaf. It took some tinkering to produce a loaf that did not crumble to pieces upon removal from the pan, or later upon slicing.

INGREDIENTS;

- 1½ cups sliced mushrooms
- 2 cloves garlic, minced
- 1 green bell pepper, diced
- ½ tsp each thyme, oregano, marjoram, tarragon, and basil
- ½ tsp salt
- ¼ tsp pepper
- 2 tbsp olive oil or butter
- 2 cups cooked brown rice or
- 4 eggs

- 1 cup Almond Pâté (see Black Olive Spread with Basil)
- ½ cup toasted cashews
- 1 cup ricotta cheese (or cottage cheeseor yogurt)
- 1 cup grated mixed cheese (see recipeintroduction)
- 2 tbsp minced parsley

PROCEDURE;

- Preheat oven to 350 degrees F. Saute mushrooms, garlic, bell pepper, and season- ings in olive oil or butter until tender.
- If using breadcrumbs instead of rice, toast 4 slices bread until brown, cool slightly, and then grind in a food processor until fine.
- Beat eggs in a large bowl, then stir in all remaining ingredients.
- Add enough ricotta or cottage cheese so that the mixture binds together firmly.
- Add more grated cheese and herbs to taste the mixture should taste strong and savory.
- Thoroughly grease two loaf pans.

- Put nut loaf into pans, smoothing the top with a spatula.
- Bake for approximately 1 hour. Loaves should be golden brown and firm to the touch. Be sure to not overcook or they will tend to be dry.
- Let sit for 5 to 10 minutes; then turn out on a wire rack to cool.
- The loaves freeze well for up to 1 month.

Vegetable-Walnut Pâté

Guests love this pâté and seem to think it tastes like real chopped liver . . .

INGREDIENTS;

1. 1 tbsp olive oil
2. ½ cup minced onion
3. ½ tsp salt
4. 1½ cups chopped green beans
5. 2 hard-boiled eggs
6. ¼ cup chopped walnuts
7. 2 tbsp white wine or lemon juice
8. 2 tbsp mayonnaise
9. ½ cup chopped parsley
10. pepper

INGREDIENTS;

- Heat oil in a small skillet. Add onion and salt and saute over medium heat until onion begins to brown, about 10 minutes.

- Add the green beans and saute until tender.
- Combine all ingredients together in a food processor and blend until a smooth paste forms. Spoon into a serving dish.

Herb-Crusted Tofu

This recipe is from Vegetarian Cooking for Everyone by Deborah Madison.

INGREDIENTS;

- 16 ounces firm tofu
- 1 cup dried breadcrumbs
- ½ cup grated Parmesan
- 1 tbsp chopped parsley
- 1 tsp dried basil or marjoram
- ½ tsp dried thyme
- ½ tsp dried savory
- 1 egg, beaten with 2 tablespoons milk or soy milk
- olive oil for frying

PROCEDURE;

1. Slice the tofu into about 1/3-inch-thick pieces, then across to form triangles.
2. Set the triangles on paper towels to drain.
3. Meanwhile, combine the breadcrumbs, cheese, and herbs in a shallow dish.

4. Dip each tofu triangle into the egg mixture and then the breadcrumb mixture, coating both sides.
5. Film a skillet with olive oil.
6. When hot, add the tofu and fry on both sides over medium heat until golden and crisp, about 10 to 12 minutes.

MYSTICAL APPLE MARTINI

INGRDIENTS;

1. 2 oz. Unsweetened dark chocolate,chopped
2. 1 tsp almond extract
3. 2 cups unsweetened coconut flakes
4. 2 oz. butter
5. 1 cups unsweetened shredded coconut
6. 2 tbsp powdered Stevia
7. 3/4 cup coconut cream
8. 1 tbsp almond butter

PROCEDURE;

- Let's start with something simple. Gather all the ingredients at one place.prefer kitchen.
- Please line the baking sheet with a parchment paper & you should then set it away.
- Okay, this one is a major step.
- Put the almond butter, butter & chocolate in a saucepan over low flame.
- Stir until melted and thoroughly mixed.
- Combine the almond extract, powdered Stevia& coconut cream

- Mix the coconut flakes & shredded coconut into the saucepan, then with draw from the flame.
- One thing remains to be done now.
- Using a tablespoon to scoop the mixture from the saucepan to the parchment paper to form bite sized pieces.
- Please place the baking sheet in the freezer & then freeze for at least 3 hours, or maybe until firm.
- 11.Smell the aroma and now serve and enjoy!!!

BUTTERY ALMOND BLAST

INGREDIENTS;

1. 2 tbsp butter
2. 1 tsp vanilla extract
3. 2 tbsp coconut oil
4. 4 tbsp erythritol
5. 1 cup heavy cream
6. 1 cup shredded coconut flakes, unsweetened
7. 1 cup almonds, toasted
8. 1 coconut cream
9. 2 tbsp coconut flour
10. 1/4 cup chia seeds
11. 1 tsp liquid stevia

PROCEDURE;

- Assemble all the ingredients at one place.
- The almonds are to be grounded in a food processor till a mealy texture is attained.

- Combine one teaspoon of coconut oil with the almond along with two tablespoons of erythritol& then continue running the food processor to make the almond butter.
- Now we can proceed to the next most important step.
- Now please heat the butter in pan till it becomes brown in color or something similar & then combine the heavy cream along with erythritol, stevia & you may then add vanilla extract.
- The mixture has to become bubbly and then add the almond butter while continuing stirring.
- As the almond butter is being incorporated, grind the chia seeds & then toast them along with coconut flakes for a few minutes.
- One thing remains to be done now.
- Mix all of them in the almond butter mixture along with coconut cream, coconut oil,& add coconut flour and spread it in a square dish.
- Now keep in the fridge for at least 1 hour or so& you may then cut intosmaller squares to serve.
- Finally, we've finished it. Enjoy!!

CUTE BACON AVOCADO BREAKFAST MUFFINS

If you want to eat your breakfast like a king Then this is the iconic recipe you're looking for.

INGREDIENTS;

1. 1/2cup Flaxseed meal
2. 1/4 tsp Red chili flakes
3. 2 minced Garlic
4. 1 ½ to 2tbsps Lemon juice
5. BlackPepper
6. 4 large eggs
7. 2 tsp, dried Chives
8. 2tsp, dried Cilantro
9. 2 tbsp Psyllium husk powder
10. 5 oz. Cheddar cheese
11. 3 tbsps, organic Butter
12. 1/2-1 cup Almond flour
13. 1tsp Baking powder
14. 2, cubed Avocados
15. 5 slices Bacon
16. 2 Coconut milk

17.   Salt
18.   2 Spring onions

PROCEDURE;

- Assemble all the ingredients at one place.
- Add flour, spices, eggs, lemon juice, flaxseed meal & coconut milk to a bowl.
- Blend until thoroughly blended.
- Now we can go ahead to the next most important step.
- Heat a skillet & then cook bacon till crispy then add the butter & avocado.
- Combine mixture to batter in a bowl& then mix.
- Set oven to 350° F and grease cupcake molds.
- One thing remains to be done now.
- Now you should add batter to molds and bake for 26 to 28 minutes.
- Take out from oven and then allow it cool before removing from mold.
- Finally, we've finished it. Enjoy!!!

ALMOND AND VANILLA SMOOTHIE

This smoothie tastes like vanilla cake batter and is perfect for either breakfast or a post workout snack.
The flavor of course will depend on the brand and type of protein powder and other ingredients that you use, so I gave you a photo of what I use below. In general, always look for high-quality and mindfully sourced ingredients without artificial colors, flavors or fillers. I always use vegan pea protein, too.

INGREDIENTS;

- 1 tbsp coconut oil
- 1 tsp pure vanilla extract
- 1 tbsp almonds,minced
- 1 cup coconut milk
- 1 tsp stevia
- 2 tbsp protein powder
- 1 cup of water

PROCEDURE;

1, Let's start with something simple. Gather all the ingredients at one place. I prefer kitchen.

2, Now please place the ingredients in a mixer or blender and pulse to mix. Now you can serve cold.

3, Finally, we've finished it. Enjoy!!

Keto Breakfast Cereal with Almond Milk

Make this simple, nutty, low-carb cinnamon cereal ahead so you'll have a quick-and-easy breakfast for busy mornings. Or, take it along for a quick, crunchy snack on the road. Without the almond milk have it and enjoy your morning.

INGREDIENTS;

- 1 cup almond flour
- 2 tbsp sunflower seeds
- 1 tbsp golden flax meal
- 1 tsp ground cinnamon
- 1 tsp vanilla extract
- ¼ tsp salt
- 2 tbsp water
- 1 tbsp butter

Serving

- with almond milk

PROCEDURE;

11. Preheat oven to 350°F
12. Blend together almond flour, sunflower seeds, flax meal, cinnamon, and salt in a bowl or preferably in a food processor to finely chop the sunflower seeds.
13. If using a food processor, pulse in the water and coconut oil until dough forms. If blending by hand, stir the liquid ingredients into dry ingredients to form a dough.
14. Put the dough ball on a sheet of parchment paper and press flat. Cover with another sheet of parchment paper and roll dough to about 1/8 to 1/16" (3 mm) thickness.
15. Put on cutting board, remove top parchment paper, and cut into 1" (2.5 cm) squares using a pizza cutter or knife.
16. With the parchment paper still on the bottom, transfer the cut dough onto a baking sheet. Bake until edges are brown and crisp (about 10-15 minutes). Allow cooling on a rack then separate squares into individual pieces.
17. Serve plain for snacking or enjoy in a bowl with almond milk or other low-carb milk.

Keto smoked salmon sandwich on spiced pumpkin bread

Smoked salmon and creamy scrambled eggs on spiced pumpkin bread it's a culinary match made in heaven! This Keto sandwich is ideal for a holiday breakfast or brunch with friends anytime. It's sure to impress and super easy to prepare.

INGREDIENTS;

Spicy pumpkin bread

- 2 tbsp pumpkin pie spice
- 1 tbsp baking powder
- 1 tsp salt
- 2 tbsp ground psyllium husk powder
- ½ cup flaxseed
- 1¼ cups almond flour
- ¼ cup coconut flour

- 1/3 cup chopped walnuts
- 1/3 cup pumpkin seeds + extra for topping
- 3 large eggs
- ½ cup unsweetened apple sauce
- ¼ cup coconut oil
- 14 oz. pumpkin puree
- 1 tbsp butter for greasing the pan

Toppings

- 4 eggs
- 2 tbsp whipping cream
- 1 tbsp butter for frying
- salt and pepper
- 1 pinch chili flakes
- 2 tbsp butter
- ½ cup leafy greens
- 3 oz. smoked salmon
- 1 tbsp fresh chives (optional)

PROCEDURE;

Spicy pumpkin bread

7. Preheat the oven to 350°F and grease a bread pan, 8.5" (about 11 x 21 cm), with butter or oil.
8. Mix together all dry ingredients in a bowl.
9. Stir together egg, apple sauce, pumpkin puree, and oil in a separate bowl and mix into a smooth batter with the dry ingredients.
10. Scoop the batter into the bread pan and sprinkle a tablespoon of pumpkin seeds on top.
11. Bake on lower rack for 30-40 minutes. If a toothpick inserted in the center comes out clean, it's done. You can also test for doneness by pressing lightly in the center of the loaf. If it feels firm then the bread is fully baked.

Building the sandwich

9. Whisk together eggs and cream in a bowl. Add salt and pepper to taste.
10. Melt the butter in a frying pan on medium-high heat. Pour in the egg mixture and stir until blended and cooked through. Remove from heat.
11. Add chili and mix. Use whatever you have at home already tabasco, dried chili flakes, or fresh finely chopped chili.
12. Toast two slices of the spicy low-carb pumpkin bread, or another low-carb bread.
13. Apply a thick layer of butter.
14. Put a few lettuce leaves and the scrambled eggs on top, then add the salmon and some finely chopped chives.

Tuna stuffed avocado

For a Keto healthy breakfast with no eggs, Grab a spoon and dig into this quick and easy budget-friendly keto breakfast that will keep you satisfied for hours! Prepare the creamy filling in advance and keep it in the fridge until serving for the ultimate fuss-free morning.

INGREDIENTS;

- 2 avocado halved lengthwise, seed removed.
- 5 oz. tuna in water, drained
- ¼ cup mayonnaise
- 1 celery stalk, finely chopped
- 2¾ tbsp shallots finely chopped
- salt and pepper, to taste
- 1 tbsp fresh chives, finely chopped (optional)

PROCEDURE;

12. In a small bowl, mix together the tuna, mayonnaise, celery, and onion, until well mixed. Season with salt and pepper, to taste.
13. For serving, top each avocado half with equal amounts of tuna filling, and garnish with chives.
14. Instead of tuna, you can also use chopped cooked chicken, ham, or salmon to make this delicious on-the-go keto breakfast

Low-carb Vegan Vanilla Protein Shake

Healthy, protein-packed, and dairy-free, this delicious and filling creamy vanilla shake is great for a fast start to your day. Just blend and go! Or, with this shake as the base, try different tasty additions to the mix to shake up your tastebuds.Use this vanilla shake recipe as a base and try adding these ingredients for different versions:

INGREDIENTS;

- ½ cup coconut milk
- ½ cup almond milk
- 1 tbsp butter
- 1 oz. frozen cauliflower rice,
- 4 tbsp pea protein powder (unflavored)
- ½ tsp cinnamon powder
- 1 tsp vanilla

PROCEDURE;

19. Put all the ingredients into a blender or food processor and blend until smooth.
20. Pour into a tall glass and enjoy

Use this vanilla shake recipe as a base and try adding these ingredients for different versions:

- Cocoa powder
- Fresh mint and spinach
- Brewed espresso or strong black coffee
- Raspberries
- Blueberries
- Avocado

Low-carb Ginger and Licorice Granola

Ginger and licorice make their mark on this yummy, simple to prepare granola. Serve it with full-fat Greek yogurt for a filling low-carb meal Decadence, indeed!

INGREDIENTS;
- 1 egg white
- 4 cup chopped almonds
- 3 tbsp sesame seeds
- 2 oz. butter or coconut oil
- ¾ cup finely shredded coconut
- ¾ cup almond flour
- 2 tsp licorice powder
- 2 tsp ground ginger
- 1 pinch salt

For serving
- 4 cups Greek yogurt
- 1 cup fresh blueberries

PROCEDURE;
1. Preheat oven to 350°F
2. Whip the egg white until fluffy.
3. Mix in the dry ingredients and the chopped almonds.
4. Work in the butter with your fingers until the texture is smooth and the dough is a single clump.
5. Spread the granola on the baking sheet in chunks. Place in the oven for 18-20 minutes.
6. Carefully turn every three minutes. The nuts should become crispy without burning. It will take about 20 minutes.
7. Store in the fridge in a tightly sealed container.
8. Serve with Greek yogurt and berries.

Keto French Toast

Who doesn't like a cozy brunch with some French toast? We've adapted this popular classic to fit all Keto needs. We're not skimping on the butter or cinnamon either. Enjoy!

INGREDIENTS;

Mug bread

- 1 tsp butter
- 2 tbsp almond flour
- 2 tbsp coconut flour
- 1½ tsp baking powder
- 1 pinch salt
- 2 large eggs
- 2 tbsp heavy cream

Batter

- 2 large eggs
- 2 tbsp heavy cream
- ½ tsp cinnamon powder
- 1 pinch salt
- 3 tbsp butter

PROCEDURE;

1. Grease a large mug or glass dish with a flat bottom with butter.
2. Mix together all dry ingredients in the mug with a fork or spoon. Add in the egg and stir in the cream. Mix well until smooth and make sure there are no lumps.
3. Microwave on high (approximately 700 watts) for 2 minutes. Check if the bread is done in the middle – if not, microwave for another 15-30 seconds.
4. Let cool and remove from the mug. Slice in half.
5. In a bowl whisk together the eggs, cream and cinnamon with a pinch of salt. Pour over the bread slices and let them get soaked. Turn them around a few times so the bread slices absorb as much of the egg mixture as possible.
6. Fry in plenty of butter and serve immediately.

7. If you don't want to measure the dry ingredients every time, prepare your own baking mix ahead. Take 10 tablespoons (150 ml) almond flour, 10 tablespoons (150 ml) coconut flour, 1 teaspoon salt and 2 1/2 tablespoons baking powder. Then you have the dry mix ready for 10 pieces.

Keto Green Smoothies

INGREDIENTS;

- 2 cups spinach(kale)
- 10 almonds (raw)
- 2 brazil nuts
- 1 cup coconut milk (unsweetened from refrigerated cartons not cans)
- 1 scoop Amazing Grass Greens Powder or barley

PROCEDURE;

- Place the spinach, almonds, brazil nuts, and coconut milk into the <u>blender</u> first.
- Blend until pureed.
- Add in the rest of the ingredients and blend well.
- serve and enjoy

Cauliflower Tabouli (Tabbouleh) Salad

INGREDIENTS;

18. 100 g (3.5 oz) cauliflower florets
19. 2 Tablespoons parsley, finely diced
20. 3 mint leaves, finely diced
21. 2 cherry tomatoes, dice
22. 1 slice lemon diced
23. 1 tbsp <u>olive oil</u>
24. Salt and pepper to taste

PROCEDURE;

- Food process the cauliflower florets to form a couscous like texture
- Make sure the florets and the food processor is dry to prevent a mash from forming instead.
- Mix the food processed cauliflower florets with the finely diced herbs, tomatoes, lemon slice, olive oil, and salt and pepper to taste.

BREAKFAST MUFFINS

INGREDIENTS;

- 3 cups <u>almond flour</u>
- 1 cup bacon bits
- ½ cup butter
- 4 eggs
- 2 tsp lemon juice
- thyme
- 1 tsp <u>baking soda</u>
- ½ tsp <u>salt</u> (optional)

PROCEDURE;

12. 1. Preheat oven to 350°F
13. Melt the Butter in a mixing bowl
14. Add in the almond flour and baking soda.
15. Add in the eggs.
16. Add in the lemon thyme (use other herbs if you prefer) and the salt.
17. Mix everything together well.
18. Lastly, add in the bacon bits.
19. Line a muffin pan with muffin liners. Spoon the mixture into the muffin pan (¾ full).
20. Bake for 18-20 minutes until a toothpick comes out clean when you insert it into a muffin.
21. Serve and enjoy!!!

Matcha Smoothie Bowl

INGREDIENTS;

15. tsp matcha powder
16. 1 scoop greens powder (optional)
17. 8 oz (240 ml) regular Greek yogurt
18. 1 tbsp chia seeds
19. 1 tbsp goji berries
20. 1 tbsp coconut flakes
21. 1 tbsp cacao nibs
22. Stevia to taste (optional)

PROCEDURE;

- 1. Blend the matcha powder with the yogurt.
- Add in stevia to sweeten it if you want.
- Pour the smoothie into a bowl.
- Top with the chia seeds, goji berries, coconut flakes, and cacao nibs
- Enjoy with a spoon.

Ghee & Coconut Coffee

INGREDIENTS;

15. ½ tbsp (7 g) <u>ghee</u>
16. ½ tbsp (7 g) <u>coconut oil</u>
17. 1-2 cups (240-480 ml) of whatever coffee you like (or black or rooibos tea)
18. 1 tbs (15 ml) almond milk or coconut milk

PROCEDURE;

- Put the ghee, coconut oil, almond milk (or coconut milk), and the coffee into a blender.
- Blend for 5-10 seconds. The coffee turns a foamy, creamy color.
- Pour it into your favorite coffee cup and enjoy!
- If you don't have a blender, then try using a <u>milk frother</u>

KETO CRÈME FRUITY

"*Seasonal fruit you prefer can be added here, to taste.*"

INGREDIENTS;

21. 1 tub of plain Greek yogurt
22. 2 tbsp of toasted almond flakes
23. 2 tbsp of toasted coconut flakes
24. 6 tbsp of fruit jelly, any flavor of choice can be used

PROCEDURE;

- Spoon 3 tablespoons of the fruit jelly into each serving bowl.
- Add half of the Greek yogurt into each serving bowl.
- Top with coconut flakes and almond flakes.
- Serve and enjoy!!!

YUMMY BERRIES WITH COCONUT CREAM

"Use seasonally available berries!"

INGREDIENTS;

- 4 cups of fresh berries, any choice, plain or mixed
- 5 leaves of fresh mint, and some more for garnish
- 1 can of coconut cream
- 2 tsp of vanilla extract
- 1 tsp of honey

PROCEDURE;

- Wash and drain the berries then divide into serving bowls.
- Chop the fresh mint finely and sprinkle over the berries.
- Open the can of chilled coconut milk.
- Use a spoon to scoop out the contents into a mixing bowl.
- Discard any juice or save it for another dish.
- Add the vanilla extract.

- Using a hand mixer, slowly beat the coconut cream.
- After around 1 minute just add the honey for sweetness (optional).
- Continue to mix until the coconut cream starts to become fluffy.
- Spoon over the berries and serve immediately.
- Garnish with the extra mint if required.

Old Tale's Bacon Cheddar & Chive Omelet

INGREDIENTS;

- 2 slices of cooked Bacon
- 2 large sized egg
- Pepper if needed
- 1 ounce Cheddar Cheese
- 2 stalks of Chive
- 1 tsp Bacon Fat
- Salt as needed

DIRECTION;

1. The first step is to make sure that all of the listed ingredients are prepared.
2. This step is important. Once done, then take a pan & place it over medium low heat
3. Now pour in the bacon fat alongside the eggs & season them with pepper, salt & chive

4. Once the edges start to brown, add in your bacon at the center & let it cook properly for 30 to 40 seconds before turning off down the stove

5. One thing remains to be done. Pour in the cheese on the top & fold the edges on top of the cheese similar to a burrito

6. Finally flip it & gently warm the other side, & you are done! Being lucky is definitely better. 1 serving

Salad For Early Morning

INGREDIENTS;

- 1 cup of water
- 1 sliced up avocado
- 1 cup of sour cream
- 1.5 tsp garlic powder
- 3 diced up tomatoes
- 1 tsp of black pepper
- 1 whole piece of chicken
- 3 cup of baby spinach

PROCEDURE;

1. The first step is to open up you're the lid of your instant pot & pour in water in your inner pot
2. Then toss in your chicken
3. Set the instant pot on poultry mode & let it cook at high pressure for 30 to 35 minutes
4. This step is important. While that is being cooked, prepare your salad by taking a bowl & toss in the tomatoes, spinach, avocado & finely mix it
5. Toss in your sour cream alongside garlic powder, sprinkled with black pepper

6. Now by this time, the chicken should be ready. Open up your instant pot & bring it out, only to cut it finely

7. Finally once cut up, pour in your dressing & serve it warm over your prepared salad. The speed matters.

Century Caprese Salad

INGREDIENTS;

25. 1 piece of Fresh Tomato
26. 1/3 a cup of chopped up Fresh Basil
27. Salt to taste
28. 2 to 3 tbsp Olive oil
29. 6 ounce Mozzarella Cheese
30. Cracked Black Pepper

PROCEDURE;

1. Take a food processor & pulse up your freshly chopped up basil leaves with 2 tablespoon of Olive Oil & turn into a fine paste
2. Then slice up your tomatoes into ¼ inch slices
3. This step is important. Cut up your Mozzarella into 1 ounce slices
4. Now assemble your Caprese salad by dishing out layers of tomato, basil leaves & mozzarella
5. One thing remains to be done. Season it up with some extra olive oil, pepper & salt as needed

Ham & Mushroom Scramble

INGREDIENTS;

- 2 slices ham
- 3 eggs
- 1.5 Tbsp coconut oi
- ½ cup spinach
- 4 bella mushrooms
- ¼ cup red bell peppers
- Salt & pepper

PROCEDURE;

1. Chop the ham & vegetables.
2. Then pour ½ tablespoon of coconut oil into a pan & sauté the ham & vegetables
3. This step is important. Crack the eggs into a bowl & whisk well. Pour the remain- ing ½ tablespoon of coconut oil into another pan & cook the scramble the eggs over medium heat.
4. Now stir the eggs constantly until they cook, & then add salt & pepper to taste.
5. Pour the sautéed ham & vegetables over the eggs & mix.
6. Finally serve hot and enjoy!!!

Mini-ham Quiches

INGREDIENTS;

- 2 ounces Swiss cheese
- 4 slices of bacon, cooked
- 6 slices ham
- 5 eggs
- 1 tbsp unsweetened almond milk
- 1/4 tsp salt
- 1/4 tsp pepper
- 1/4 tsp onion powder
- non-stick cooking spray

PROCEDURE;

1. Preheat the oven to 350°F. Dice the cheese and bacon. In a small bowl, whisk together eggs, milk, salt, pepper, and onion powder.
2. Spray a 6-cup muffin pan and line each cup with one slice of the deli ham.
3. Evenly distribute the cheese and bacon to each cup, and then fill each cup with the egg mixture until it fills each cup but be careful it does not overflow. You may want to use a measuring cup to help control

the liquid as you fill them.
4. Bake for 20 minutes. Cool slightly before serving.

Crepes with Nut Butter and Whipped Cream

INGREDIENTS;

Nut Butter:

23. 3/4 cup roasted, husked hazelnuts
24. 2 tbsp Xylitol or equivalent measurement of the zero carb sweetener
25. 2 tbsp cocoa powder
26. 1/8 tsp salt
27. 1/2 tsp vanilla extract
28. 2 tbsp coconut oil

Crepes;

- 1/2 cups almond flour
- 2 tbsp Xylitol or equivalent measurement of the zero carb sweetener
- 4 ounces cream cheese brick
- 4 eggs
- 1/8 tsp salt
- 3 tsp salted butter

Whipped Cream:

19. 1-1/2 cup heavy cream
20. 3/4 tsp vanilla extract
21. 3 tbsp Xylitol or equivalent measurement of the zero carb sweetener

PROCEDURE;

Note:
- You can store the crepes in the refrigerator after they have completely cooled (you might want to put parchment paper or plastic wrap between each one).
- You can also store the nut butter in the refrigerator for a couple of weeks.
- Once whipped, the whipping cream does not keep well, but you can keep it as a liquid in the fridge and then whip 1/4 cup per serving as you need it.
- Finely ground nuts in a food processor. While continuing to grind, slowly add cocoa powder, salt, vanilla, and melted coconut oil until it reaches the desired con- sistency.
- If you want thinner nut butter, you can add up to 1 additional tablespoon of coconut oil for a total of

3 tablespoons.

- Use a hand immersion blender to combine all the crepe ingredients except the butter in a 1-quart measuring cup or small pitcher.
- Using a crepe-maker or an 8" skillet, heat the pan over medium-low heat and use about ¼ teaspoon of butter to coat the pan.
- If you are using a crepe-maker, follow the provided instructions.
- Otherwise, pour 1/8 cup batter into the pan, quickly pick up the skillet, and swirl the pan to distribute the batter across the entire bottom of the pan.
- This may take some practice. It takes about 10 seconds for the crepe to finish cooking on one side.
- Once it is done, flip the crepe and cook another 10 seconds on the other side. Remove the crepe from the pan and place it on a plate.
- Continue making crepes until you are out of batter. Whisk (by hand or with a stand mixer and the appropriate attachment) the cream, vanilla, and sweetener until stiff.
- Place 1 crepe on a flat surface and spread 1 tablespoon of the nut butter on top of it. Spread 1

tablespoon of whipped cream on top of the nut butter and roll.
- When you have finished making the crepes, evenly distribute the left-over whipped cream on top of the crepe rolls.

Strawberry-Coconut Porridge

INGREDIENTS;

25. 3/4 cup water
26. 2 tablespoons ground flax seeds
27. 2 tablespoons coconut flour
28. 1/8 teaspoon kosher salt
29. 1 egg, well-beaten
30. 2 teaspoons butter
31. 1 tablespoon coconut milk
32. 1/4 cup strawberries
33. Greased loaf pans

PROCEDURE;

- In a medium saucepan, combine water, flax seeds, flour, and salt.
- Stirring frequently, heat on medium-high until the porridge thickens slightly.
- Remove from heat. Whisk in the egg, slowly until the porridge thickens and the egg is well combined.
- Serve in a bowl topped with the butter, coconut milk, and strawberries.

TANTALIZING CHICKEN SALAD WITH BACON

INGREDIENTS;

9. 1 large egg
10. 4 oz. of chicken breast, skin and bone removed, sliced
11. 1 cup of spinach, washed and dried
12. 2 strips of bacon, cut into small pieces
13. 1/4 of an avocado, peeled, seeded and diced
14. 1 tbsp of olive oil
15. 1/2 a tsp of white vinegar
16. pinch salt and pepper, to taste

PROCEDURE;

- Boil the egg for 10 minutes in boiling water, then cool in cold water.
- Peel egg and then chop or slice.

- Heat a skillet over medium heat, add the chicken slices and cook for 3 minutes, or until cooked through.
- Move the chicken to the side and then add the bacon pieces, cook until your desired crispiness.
- In a mixing bowl, rip the spinach leaves then add the bacon, the chicken, and the chopped egg.
- Add the diced avocado, then drizzle with vinegar and olive oil.
- Season with salt and pepper, to taste.
- Toss together to coat all of the ingredients.
- Transfer to a serving plate.

GORGEOUS TUNA SALAD WITH AVOCADO

"Chicken works well here too, especially if you don't like tuna."

INGREDIENTS;

- 4 oz. can of tuna in brine or oil, drained
- 1 stalk of celery, diced
- 1/2 an avocado, peeled, seeded, and diced
- 2 tsp mayonnaise
- 1 tsp mustard
- 1/2 tsp lemon juice
- salt and pepper, to taste
- 1 egg, hard-boiled, peeled & chopped

PROCEDURE;

- In a mixing bowl, add the tuna, celery, and avocado.
- Add the mayonnaise, mustard, and the lemon juice.
- Add the egg to the tuna salad.
- Season with salt and black pepper.
- Mix well until combined.
- Serve and enjoy!!!

AMAZING ASIAN BEEF AND COLESLAW

INGRDIENTS;

8. 1 tbsp of olive oil
9. 2 cloves of garlic, crushed
10. 1/2 a lb. of ground beef
11. 5 oz. of coleslaw salad mix
12. 1 tbsp of low-sodium soy sauce
13. salt and pepper, to taste
14. 1 teaspoon of sesame seeds
15. 2 spring onions, chopped

PROCEDURE;

- In a wok or medium skillet, add a small amount of olive oil and heat over a medium heat.
- Heat the olive oil and add the crushed garlic. Cook until fragrant.
- Add the ground beef and brown until meat is cooked through, around 5 to 10 minutes.

- Stir while cooking and break up any lumps with a wooden spoon.
- When cooked, add in the coleslaw and stir to mix.
- Add in the olive oil and the low-sodium soy sauce.
- Stir and cook for around 5 minutes until the coleslaw mix starts towilt.
- Season with salt and black pepper, to your taste.
- Serve with a sprinkle of sesame seeds and spring onion on the top and enjoy!!!

SHRIMP WITH SWEET AND SPICY CHICKEN

INGRDIENTS;

- 2 chicken breasts, boneless and skinless
- 20 large shrimp, peeled
- 1/2 a cup of mushrooms, sliced
- 2 handfuls of spinach
- 1/4 of a cup of mayonnaise
- 2 tsp of sriracha sauce
- 1 tbsp of coconut oil
- 2 tsp of fresh lime juice
- salt and black pepper, to taste
- 1 tsp of garlic powder
- 1/2 tsp of crushed red pepper
- 1/2 tsp of paprika
- 1/2 tsp of honey
- 1 spring onion, finely chopped

PROCEDURE;

1. Tenderize chicken slices between plastic wrap until it is of a 1-inch thickness.
2. Season with sea salt, black pepper, and garlic powder.
3. In a skillet over medium heat, add the coconut oil and chicken breasts.
4. Cook for 8 minutes and turn once. Reduce the heat and cover.
5. Add the sliced mushrooms to the chicken.
6. Add oil if required. In a mixing bowl, whisk together the mayonnaise, sriracha, and honey.
7. Heat a pot over medium-high heat, and place the shrimp in one layer.
8. Add the sauce and toss to coat. Cook for around 3 minutes until the shrimp are pink. Stir occasionally to prevent burning.
9. Remove from the heat and add the fresh lime juice and toss to cover all the shrimp.
10. Divide spinach onto serving plates with cooked mushrooms.
11. Add the chicken and shrimp, and coat with the sauce.
12. Sprinkle with chopped spring onion to garnish.

SPICED LIME STEAK AND ASPARAGUS

INGREDIENTS;
- 14 oz. of asparagus
- 1/2 a lb. of thin beef steak
- salt and black pepper, for seasoning
- olive oil, for cooking

Lime and Sriracha Sauce
- 1 lime juice
- 2 tbsp of sriracha sauce, or more to taste
- 1/2 tsp of vinegar
- salt and pepper, to taste
- 1 tbsp of olive oil

PROCEDURE;

- Place a medium skillet over medium-heat. Add a dash of olive oilFry the asparagus for around 10 minutes, toss to avoid burning.
- Season the steaks with salt and black pepper.

- Broil until cooked to your liking. Turn once.
- Remove from broiler and cover. Let the steak rest for 5 minutes.
- In a small mixing bowl, add the lime juice, vinegar and sriracha sauce.
- Add the salt and black pepper.
- Slowly pour the olive oil while whisking, to combine thoroughly.
- Slice the steaks into thin strips. Serve with fried asparagus and drizzle lime sauce over the top.

CHEESY-TOPPED BAKED PORK

INGREDIENTS;

- 1/2 a lb. of pork steaks
- 3/4 of a cup of heavy cream
- 6 oz. of creamed cheese
- 1/4 of a cup of soy flour
- a pinch salt & pepper
- 1 tsp of paprika
- 1/2 a tbsp of garlic salt
- 1/2 a cup of parmesan cheese, grated
- butter, for cooking

PROCEDURE;

- Slice pork steaks into thin strips.
- In a mixing bowl, combine the flour, salt, pepper, and the paprika.
- Coat the steak strips with the seasoned flour.
- Heat a skillet over medium-heat and add butter.
- When melted, cook the pork until brown on all sides.

- In a small pot, heat the cream and add the cream cheese, and then
- add the garlic salt with half of the parmesan cheese. Mix until well blended.
- Place pork pieces into the bottom of a small baking dish.
- Cover the strips with sauce, and with the remaining 1/4 of a cup of
- parmesan cheese sprinkled on the top.
- Bake for 20 minutes at 180 degrees C, or until golden brown.
- Divide between serving plates and serve hot.

SCRUMMY SAUSAGE PIE

INGREDIENTS

- 8 oz. of sausage
- 8 oz. of cream cheese
- 2 eggs
- 1/3 of a cup of heavy cream
- 3 cups of zucchini, shredded
- 1/4 a cup of spring onions, roughly chopped
- salt and pepper, to taste
- 3/4 of a cup of baking milk

PROCEDURE;

1. Preheat oven to 280°F
2. Preheat a medium skillet over medium-heat. Cook the sausage in their own oil until no pink remains, and until they are cooked all the way through.
3. Mix well together with the baking mix, cream, and eggs.

4. Arrange sausages in a spoke pattern in a medium baking dish.
5. Pour baking mixture around the sausages in the baking dish.
6. Add salt and pepper, to taste.
7. Cook uncovered for around 30 minutes (or until starting to brown),
                and until the mixture is set.
8. Serve immediately..

KETO LUNCH

Blackened Shrimp and Asparagus Skillet

These delicious blackened shrimp with asparagus are the perfect versatile and fast lunch meal. Flavorful, juicy shrimp team up with crisp-tender asparagus in this easy one-pan lunch everyone will crave about. Ready in few minutes, this shrimp recipe with asparagus cooks in just one pan and is low carb, and keto-friendly. Enjoy!

INGREDIENTS;

- 450g large shrimp, peeled and deveined
- 1 tsp chili flakes
- 2 tsp paprika
- 1tbsp minced onion
- 1 tsp cumin
- 1/2 tsp garlic powder
- 1 tsp salt
- 1/4 tsp freshly cracked black pepper
- 2 tbsp olive oil, divided
- 1 tbsp butter
- 700g asparagus rinsed and trimmed
- 1/4 cup vegetable broth
- 1 tbsp hot sauce, (optional)
- 1 tbsp lemon juice
- Lemon slices, red chili flakes, fresh chopped parsley, for garnish.

PROCEDURE;

13. To make the blackened shrimp and asparagus skillet: In a bowl put the shrimp, chili powder, paprika, onion powder, cumin, garlic powder, and salt and pepper. Coat well and set aside.
14. In a skillet over medium-high heat, add 1 tablespoon oil and cook seasoned shrimp on each side for 3-5 minutes or until browned and cooked through. Remove to a shallow plate and set aside.
15. In the same skillet (clean up if necessary, to remove brown bits), add 1 tablespoon olive oil and 1 tablespoon butter and reduce heat to medium. Add vegetable stock, lemon juice and sriracha and bring to a simmer. Allow the sauce to reduce a little, then add the asparagus and cook the asparagus until crisp-tender, approx. 4-6 minutes, turning the asparagus regularly to coat into the sauce.
16. Push the asparagus on the side and add blackened shrimp back to the pan. Squeeze a dash of lemon juice on top of the blackened

shrimp and asparagus. Allow reheating for 1-2 minutes then remove grilled shrimp and asparagus from heat, garnish with parsley, lemon slices, and red crushed chili pepper if you like. Serve your blackened shrimp and asparagus immediately, enjoy! You can serve the blackened shrimp and asparagus with a side of zucchini noodles, cauliflower rice, mashed potato, or just plain regular rice.

HOW TO MAKE BLACKENED SHRIMP;

- To make blackened shrimp, you can use shrimp with tails on or off.
- Buy shrimp already deveined, shelled and cleaned to save time.
- You can save time when cooking asparagus by blanching them first in boiling water for 2 minutes then soak in ice water to stop cooking. Then you can cook asparagus as per the recipe.
- If spice and shrimp leave too many brown bits, rinse and clean the skillet to avoid asparagus having a bitter taste.
- You can buy cajun blackening seasoning to save time when prepping for the recipe.

Garlic Sautéed Cabbage Kale Skillet

Delicious and packed with nutrients, this healthful blend of sautéed cabbage and kale makes a wonderful side dish for any main course or a vegetarian main on its own. Slightly caramelized onion and cabbage develop their natural sweetness for extra flavors. Low carb, Keto, paleo, vegetarian, and gluten-free, this kale and cabbage recipe is the perfect way to get your veggies in! Enjoy!

INGREDIENTS;

- 4 tbsp butter or ghee
- 2 tbsp olive oil
- 1 shallots, chopped
- 1/2 head cabbage, chopped
- 450g kale, Lacinato or dinosaur, washed, and thinly sliced)
- 2 tbsp vegetable broth
- 2 tbsp parsley, chopped

- 4 cloves garlic, minced
- 1/2 teaspoon salt and pepper, or to taste
- 1/2 tsp chili flakes, or to taste

PROCEDURE;

1. To make the cabbage and kale skillet: Heat the butter and oil in a large pan or skillet over medium-high heat. Sauté the onion until softened (about 3 minutes).
2. Add the cabbage and cook for about 4-5 minutes stirring from time to time.
3. Once the cabbage is softened and starts to caramelize on the edges, add chopped kale, garlic, salt, pepper, and red chili pepper flakes. Cook for about 8-10 minutes. Veggies must be well-browned and softened.
4. Pour in the vegetable stock to deglaze and cook for 2 minutes, to reduce the sauce slightly. Scrape the bottom of the pan with a wooden spoon to catch the delicious browned bits!
5. Cook the cabbage and kale for half a minute, until fragrant. Season with more pepper, to taste, sprinkle with parsley, and serve the Sauteed Garlic Cabbage Kale Skillet immediately. Enjoy!

Low-carb Vegan Kebab Wraps with Garlic Sauce

These colorful low-carb vegan kebab wraps are a healthy and delicious plant-based protein source. Perfect for lunch or dinner for the whole family, a low-carb twist on a Middle Eastern delicacy. The vegan kebabs freeze well, so make a double batch and put the leftovers
in the freezer for another day.

INGREDIENTS;

Vegan kebabs

- ½ cup almonds
- ½ cup pumpkin seeds
- 8 oz. mushrooms, sliced
- ½ cup light olive oil, divided
- ¾ cup pea protein powder (unflavored)
- ¼ cup chia seeds
- 1 garlic clove, crush
- 2 tbsp fresh parsley, finely chopped

- 2 tsp ground cumin
- 2 tsp onion powder
- 1 tsp ground coriander seed
- ¼ cup water
- 1 tsp salt
- ¼ tsp ground black pepper

Garlic sauce with mint

- 3 tbsp chickpea water
- 1 tbsp lemon juice
- 2 garlic cloves, crush
- 1 cup light olive oil
- 2 tsp dried mint
- ¼ tsp salt

Veggies

- 1 Romaine lettuce
- 1 cucumber, diced
- 2 tomatoes
- 1 Onion diced
- ½ cup fresh parsley, finely chopped

PROCEDURE;

Vegan kebabs

9. Preheat the oven to 350°F
10. Heat up a large dry frying pan and roast the almonds and pumpkin seeds until lightly browned and fragrant. Put them in a food processor and pulse for a couple of minutes.
11. Fry the mushrooms in a large frying pan in 1/3 of the olive oil until soft and moist.
12. Add the cooked mushrooms in the food processor together with the remaining oil and the rest of the kebab ingredients. Mix for a couple of minutes. Let sit for about 5 minutes.
13. Form the mixture into sausage-shaped kebabs. Place them on a baking sheet.
14. Bake in the oven for 20 minutes or until crispy. In the meantime, prepare the sauce and the veggies.

Garlic sauce with mint

1. Add the the liquid in a can of cooked chickpeas, lemon juice and garlic in a tall blender jar .
2. Blend on high speed with an immersion blender for about 30 seconds until frothy.
3. Add olive oil in a very slow, thin stream, while mixing on full speed. A smooth, creamy emulsion should form. Towards the end, move the immersion blender up and down to incorporate a little air to get it more fluffy.
4. Add the dried mint and salt, and combine.

Veggies

1. Cut of the end of the romaine lettuce, wash and separate the leafs.
2. Finely dice the cucumber, tomatoes, red onion and parsley. Mix together.
3. Top the romaine lettuce leafs with a kebab each, salad and garlic sauce.

Keto Zucchini Crab Melts

It's a cheesy, gooey crab melt, ketofyed! Whip up this easy Keto crab melt on top of zucchini for a satisfying lunch or a light dinner. Great for meal prep, so go ahead and make a double batch.

INGREDIENTS;

- 2 zucchini
- 1 tbsp olive oil
- ¾ cup celery stalks
- 1 red capsicum
- 12 oz. canned crab meat
- ¾ cup mayonnaise
- 1 tbsp Dijon mustard
- 1¾ cups shredded cheddar cheese
- salt and pepper

Serving

- 3 2/3 cup baby spinach
- 2 tbsp olive oil
- salt and pepper to taste

PROCEDURE;

1. Preheat the oven to 400F° Slice the zucchini lengthwise, about half an inch (1 cm) thick. Scoop out a trench in the middle of the zucchini using a spoon to make room for the filling.
2. Sprinkle the zucchini with salt. Let sit for 15-20 minutes to draw out some of the moisture.
3. Pat dry with a piece of paper towel.
4. While the zucchini is sitting, chop the capsicum and celery finely. You can also use a food processor to chop vegetables if you wish.
5. Place the zucchini slices on a baking sheet lined with parchment paper. Brush olive oil on both sides and bake for 7 minutes. Remove from oven.
6. Mix the chopped vegetables with crab meat, mayo, dijon, and cheese. Make sure all of the moisture is squeezed out of the crab meat,

otherwise it may be too loose. Season the mixture with salt and pepper to taste.
7. put the mixture onto the zucchini slices using spoon. Bake for 15-20 minutes or until the top look golden brown .
8. Serve with baby spinach and a drizzle of olive oil and enjoy!

Bagel Omelet

Enjoy the crunch of egg seasoned with sesame seeds, onion, and garlic with the rich flavors of turkey, bacon, and sun-dried tomatoes made even more dreamy with bits of cream cheese in the filling.

INGREDIENTS;

- 1 tbsp butter
- 2 large eggs
- 1 tsp bagel seasoning
- 1 oz. bacon, cooked
- 2 oz. deli turkey, chopped
- 2 tsp sun-dried tomatoes, chopped
- 2 tbsp cream cheese
-

PROCEDURE;

1. Prepare the sun-dried tomatoes, turkey, and bacon. Divide the cream cheese into small pieces. Set aside.
2. Melt the butter in a small skillet or omelet pan on low heat. Whip the eggs in a small bowl with the bagel seasoning until frothy. Pour the eggs into the skillet
3. When the egg begins to cook, add the bacon, turkey, tomatoes, and cream cheese to one side of the omelet
4. Fold the other side of the omelet on top of the filling and continue cooking to warm the filling and melt the cream cheese. Flip the omelet to warm the other side if necessary. Serve with a garnish of fresh herbs such as chives, basil, or thyme if desired.

Pork Chops with Green Beans and Garlic Butter

Juicy pork chops. Crunchy green beans. Garlic butter. Now that's what we call a one-skillet wonder. And it's Keto Lunch elegance at its finest.

INGREDIENTS;

Garlic butter

- 4tbsp butter,
- ½ tbsp garlic powder
- 1 tbsp dried parsley
- 1 tbsp lemon juice
- salt and pepper

Pork chops

- 700grams pork chops
- 2 oz. butter, for frying
- 400 grams fresh green beans
- salt and pepper

PROCEDURE;

1. Mix butter, garlic, parsley and lemon juice. Season with salt and pepper to taste. Set aside.
2. Make a few small cuts in the fat surrounding the chops to help them stay flat when frying. Season with salt and pepper.
3. In a large skillet, melt the butter over medium-high heat. Add the chops and fry for about 5 minutes on each side or until golden brown and cooked thoroughly.
4. Remove the chops from the pan and keep warm.
5. Use the same skillet and add the beans. Salt and pepper to taste. Cook over medium-high heat until the beans have a vibrant color and are slightly softened but still a bit crunchy.

6. Serve the pork chops and beans together with a spoon full of garlic butter melting on top.

Keto Pork Chops with Blue-Cheese Sauce

Mix things up a little bit! Any kind of meat, either bone-in or boneless, is delicious with this incredibly versatile meal. Try filet or chops. Try beef, pork or lamb. Even humble poultry like chicken or turkey gets kicked up a notch with this sauce. Just remember how much flavor the skin or fat of these meats brings to a dish—so definitely leave them on if you can!

Salty and savory, this blue cheese sauce dresses up the average pork chop and metaphorically takes this amazingly simple and delectable meal. Fire up your stovetop and begin cooking! Indulge

INGREDIENTS;

- 5 oz. blue cheese
- ¾ cup heavy whip cream
- 4 pork chops
- salt and pepper to taste

- 250 grams fresh green beans
- 4 tbsp butter, for frying

PROCEDURE;

1. Start by crumbling the cheese into a small pot over medium heat. Adjust heat if necessary to let it melt gently. Be careful not to let it burn. When the cheese has melted, add the cream and increase the heat a little. Let simmer for a few minutes.
2. Season the chops with salt and pepper. Fry in a skillet on medium-high heat for 2-3 minutes before flipping. Cook until internal temperature is 145°-160°F. Set aside and cover with foil for 2-3 minutes.
3. Pour the pan juices into the cheese sauce. Stir and, if needed, heat it up again. As blue cheese is often fairly salty, taste the sauce before adding any additional salt.
4. Trim and rinse the green beans. Fry them in butter for a few minutes on medium heat. Season with salt and pepper and enjoy.

Ham, Egg, and Cheese Roll-ups

INGREDIENTS;
- 6 slices ham
- 6-1.3 ounce slices of cheddar cheese
- 4 eggs
- 1 tbsp chives, finely sliced
- 1 tbsp butter
- 1/4 tsp salt
- 1-1/8 tsp of black pepper
- 1/4 tsp of onion powder
- Non-stick cooking spray
- Toothpicks (soaked in water)

PROCEDURE;
- Preheat oven to 380 F.
- Whisk together eggs, salt, onion powder, and black pepper in a medium bowl until smooth.
- Place a medium frying pan on low heat and melt the butter in it. Slowly pour the egg into the warm pan with the butter.
- Wait until the bottom of the eggs begins to cook, and then use a silicone spatula to constantly stir and agitate the eggs until they are done to your satisfaction.

- Remove the eggs from the heat immediately. Lay out the slices of ham next to each other and top with a slice of cheese.
- Evenly distribute the eggs on top of each slice of cheese. Sprinkle chives on top of eggs.
- Spray a small cooking dish with non-stick cooking spray.
- Roll the ham, egg, and cheese slices, using a soaked toothpick to secure the roll. Carefully transfer the rolls to the prepared cooking dish.
- Bake 10 minutes until the ham is browned and its edges are slightly curled.

Chicken Strips & Cauliflower Bites

INGREDIENTS;

Chicken Strips:

2 eggs

2 teaspoons Dijon mustard

1 tsp salt

1 tsp black pepper

1-1/2 cup finely grated Parmesan cheese

1/4 cup almond flour

4 tbsp cooking oil

1-pound boneless, skinless chicken breasts cut into 8 tenders or 8 pre-cut ten- ders

Cauliflower Bites:

12 ounces (about 1/2 a large head) cauliflower

4 egg yolks

3/4 cup almond flour

3/4 cup finely grated Parmesan cheese

1 tsp garlic powder

1/2 tsp salt

1/2 tsp cayenne pepper (optional)

3/4 cup butter

PROCEDURE;

- Whisk together eggs, brown mustard, salt, and pepper.
- Toss together the cheese and almond flour. Heat cooking oil on high until hot.
- Dip each tender first in the egg mixture and then in the cheese mixture.
- Place them in the oil to cook until done, approximately 5 minutes.
- Remove from oil and place on a paper towel. Break cauliflower into florets and place in a skillet with about 1/4-inch of water.
- Bring to a simmer, and then reduce heat and cover for 8 minutes.
- Drain off any remaining water and set aside to cool. Whisk together the egg yolks, garlic, salt, and cayenne pepper (if desired) in a small bowl.
- Toss the bread crumbs and cheese together in a separate bowl. Melt the butter in a skillet over medium-high heat.
- Carefully place the cauliflower florets into the egg yolk mixture a few at a time, making sure they are well coated.
- Then transfer them to the bread crumb

mixture using a slotted spoon and toss them to coat. Transfer them to the skillet with the butter and cook until brown, approximately 4 minutes.

Hot Curried Pumpkin Soup

INGREDIENTS;

1 (15-ounce) can pumpkin

1/4 cup coconut oil

1 cup onion, chopped

1 clove minced garlic

3 cups chicken broth

1 tbsp curry powder

1/2 tsp salt

1/2 tsp coriander

1/2 tsp red pepper flakes

1/2 tsp cinnamon

1/2 tsp grated ginger

1 cup coconut milk

1/4 small apple cubes

3 slices bacon, cooked

6 teaspoons sour cream

Zero carb sweetener of your choice (optional-to taste)

PROCEDURE;

1. Heat the coconut oil until melted in a Dutch oven.
2. Sauté the onions and garlic in the pot until the onions become translucent, approximately 5

minutes.
3. Add the vegetable broth, salt, and seasonings.
4. Cook on medium heat until the mixture comes to a gentle boil, and then cover and cook an additional 15-20 minutes, stir- ring occasionally.
5. Whisk together the coconut milk and pumpkin and then add this mixture to the pot. Continue cooking for another 5 minutes.
6. Taste the soup to determine if it is sweet/spicy enough for you. You can add zero carb sweetener to make the soup sweet and/or add additional curry or red pepper to increase the heat.
7. Once it is ad- justed, use a hand immersion blender to process the soup until it is smooth.
8. Divide the apple cubes into six bowls.
9. Pour 1 cup of soup in each bowl and gar- nish with 1 teaspoon sour cream and 1/2 slice of crumbled bacon.

Hot and Spicy Thai Beef Salad

INGREDIENTS;

- 4 ounces lean sirloin steak
- 2 tsp olive oil
- 1/4 tsp rice vinegar
- 1/8 tsp salt
- 1/8 tsp pepper
- 1 clove garlic
- 1/2 tsp zero carb chili paste
- 1/2 tsp lime juice
- 1-1/2 ounce spinach
- 1 ounce coleslaw mix
- 1 ounce cucumber, chopped
- 2 tsp olive oil
- 1/4 tsp rice vinegar
- 1/4 tsp salt
- 1/4 tsp pepper
- 1/8 tsp curry powder

PROCEDURE;

- The night before:
- Cut the steak into thin strips.

- In a plastic baggie, combine 2 teaspoons of the olive oil, salt, pepper, garlic, chili paste, and lime juice.
- Add the meat to this bag of marinade and seal the bag.
- Allow the meat to marinate in your refrigerator 6-24 hours. After the steak has marinated:
- Toss the spinach, coleslaw mix, and cucumber together.
- Combine the remaining olive oil, vinegar, salt, pepper, and curry powder and add this oil mixture to the salad. Tossing lightly.
- Place salad on serving plate.
- Cook steak in a small skillet over high heat until it reaches your preferred level of doneness.
- Flip half-way through cooking. Place steak on top of salad and serve.

Mushroom Pizza Bites

INGREDIENTS;

16. 4 whole portabella mushroom caps with the stems removed
17. 4-1/2 ounces mozzarella cheese cut 4 even slices
18. 8 slices pepperoni
19. 4 slices 1/4" thick a big tomato
20. 1/2 tsp salt
21. 1/4 tsp pepper
22. 2 tsp oregano
23. 1 tbsp basil
24. 1 clove garlic
25. 2 tbsp olive oil

PROCEDURE;

- Preheat broiler.
- Place Portobello mushroom caps upside down on a broiler-safe pan.
- Toss stir the oil and garlic together in a small, spouted measuring cup and drizzle oil mix-ture over the mushrooms.
- Place one slice of mozzarella on top of each

mushroom and then top that with two slices of pepperoni and a tomato slice. Sprinkle oregano, basil, salt, and pepper on top of the tomato slices.
- Broil 6-8 minutes being careful not to overcook. The cheese should be melted.

Sesame Crusted Tuna

INGREDIENTS;

- 2 tuna steaks 4-1/2 ounces each steak
- 1/8 teaspoon salt
- 1/8 teaspoon ground ginger
- 2 tablespoons whole sesame seeds
- 2 teaspoons olive oil
- 2 teaspoons soy sauce
- 3 tablespoons store mayonnaise
- 1 teaspoon Sriracha sauce or your favorite zero carb hot chili sauce

PROCEDURE;

17. Place the tuna steaks on a flat, clean surface and sprinkle with salt and ginger.
18. Place the olive oil in a skillet over medium heat.
19. Place the sesame seeds on a plate and gently press all sides of the tuna steaks into the seeds to coat the steaks.

20. Once coated, add the soy sauce to the oil and cook the steaks in the mixture, covered, until the desired level of doneness is reached.
21. Flip steaks at least once half-way through cooking.
22. Seeds should be at least golden in color when the steaks are done.
23. Whisk together the mayonnaise and hot sauce. Serve each of the steaks with half of the mayonnaise sauce.

Chicken and Bacon Salad

INGREDIENTS;

- 4 slices bacon, cooked, cut into 1" slices
- 1 cup rotisserie chicken, cut in 1" cubes
- 1/2 cup cheddar cheese, grated
- 2 tsp chives, finely chopped
- 2 scallions each 3" long, thinly sliced
- 2 tbsp sour cream
- 2 tbsp olive oil
- 2 cups Romaine lettuce, chopped
- 1/8 tsp salt
- 1/8 tsp black pepper

PROCEDURE;
- Toss lettuce, scallions, and chives.
- Add olive oil, chicken, bacon, and cheese.
- Mix again to evenly distribute.
- Sprinkle cheese and salt and pepper on top.
- Spoon the sour cream on to the top.
- Split evenly into two bowls and serve.

Beef and Cauliflower Spicy Pan

INGREDIENTS;

- 1 lb. ground beef
- 1 tbsp butter
- 4 pastured eggs
- ½ cup chopped shallots
- 2.5 tsp minced garlic
- 2 cups cauliflower florets
- 1 tbsp chopped parsley
- ½ tsp black pepper
- ½ cup water
- 1.5 tsp coconut aminos
- ¾ tsp cumin
- 1 tsp salt
- ½ cup diced avocado
- 2.5 tbsp sliced jalapeno

PROCEDURE;

- Preheat an oven to about 250°F & prepare a disposable aluminum pan.

- Coat with cooking spray & set aside. This step is important.
- Place cauliflower florets in a food processor then process until smooth. Set aside.
- Preheat a skillet over medium heat then place butter in it.
- Now once the butter is melted, stir in chopped shallots & minced garlic then sauté until wilted & aromatic.
- Add ground beef to the skillet then season with salt, pepper, coconut aminos, & cumin.
- Cook until the ground beef is no longer pink.
- Then pour water over the ground beef then add cauliflower crumbles to the skillet.
- Stir well & cook until the water is completely absorbed into the beef & cauli- flower.
- Remove from heat.
- Please transfer the cooked beef & cauliflower to the prepared aluminum pan & spread evenly.
- Crack the egg & drop over the beef & cauliflower then top with diced avocado, sliced jalapeno, & chopped parsley.
- Then bake the beef & cauliflower pan for approximately about 10 to 15 minutes or until the eggs are set & the top is lightly golden brown.

- One thing remains to be done now. Once it is done, remove the aluminum pan from the oven & let the beef & cauliflower pan rest for a few minutes.
- Finally serve & enjoy.

Meat Lover's Stir Fry

INGREDIENTS;

10. 2 cups spinach
11. 1/3 cup sugar-free tomato sauce
12. 3 good quality sausages
13. 1/3 cup parmesan cheese
14. 2 ½ tbsp red wine
15. 1 ½ tbsp butter, salted
16. 1 ½ tbsp garlic, minced
17. Dash of red pepper flakes
18. 2 cups broccoli florets
19. pinch ofsalt and pepper

PROCEDURE;

- Cut your sausages into bite-sized pieces.
- Bring a large pot with enough water to cover the broccoli to a boil.
- This step is important. Put a large pan with the sausage slices over high heat.
- Once they start sizzling, reduce heat & continuously stir until they are cooked through.

- Now once the pot of water comes to a boil, add the broccoli & cook to your de- sired level of tenderness.
- Then, drain the water & set aside.
- By now, your sausages should have browned, am I right
- Awesome, now move them to one half of the pan & put the butter in the other half.
- Once the butter starts to brown, add the garlic & let cook until it has browned as well.
- Stir the sausages into the garlic butter until they are evenly coated.
- Please transfer the broccoli to the sausages & stir until the broccoli also has an even coating of garlic butter.
- Once all ingredients are well combined, add in the tomato sauce, red wine, pep- per, red pepper flakes, & salt.
- Stir until thoroughly incorporated.
- Now you can add the spinach. Give it a stir as the leaves wilt to incorporate it with the rest of the mix.
- Once the spinach has wilted, let the mixture simmer for about 5 to 10 minutes or until the wine cooks down.

- Finally transfer to serving plates, sprinkle with the parmesan cheese, & dig in!

Keto Chicken Salad

INGREDIENTS;

- 12 green/red seedless grapes
- Pepper & Salt to taste
- 3 tbsp. mayonnaise/more as needed to moisten
- ½ c. chopped celery
- 1 ½ c. diced cooked chicken breast
- 1 spring onion

PROCEDURE;

1. Combine the celery, diced chicken, & spring onion with the mayonnaise.
2. This step is important. Sprinkle with the pepper & salt adding more mayo if needed
3. Chop the grapes into halves & mix in to combine. If desired, add a dash of curry powder.
4. You can use it as a filling for rolls, buns, or sliced bread, rolls.
5. One thing remains to be done now. Make it even healthier & add it to heaps of lettuce leaves or greens.

6. Finally you can even add this to one of your mason jar salads. This is different, isn't it?

King sized Creamy Mushroom with Chicken

INGREDIENTS;

- 3 tbsps. butter unsalted
- 2 chicken cutlets
- salt, pepper to taste
- 1 big shallot
- 5 cremini mushrooms
- ½ tsp. dried thyme
- 1/3 cup fat canned coconut milk

PROCEDURE;

- Heat your skillet to medium heat.
- Slice up your mushrooms & onion.
- This step is important. Once it's hot, add the butter.
- When melted, add in the mushrooms & a bit of salt.
- Sauté until brown; then it's the onion's turn.
- Keep stirring for about 5 to 10 minutes & then remove the mix.
- Then add the remaining butter & melt it.

- One thing remains to be done now. Season your chicken with salt & pepper & thyme & then place it in the skillet.
- Finally cook each side for about 5 to 10 mins. Finally, place your mix back & pour the coconut milk right over it.
- Serve and enjoy!!!

Pinnacle Monterey Mug Melt

Here's another easy idea that you might enjoy if you liked the Keto mug lasagna. This time we'll layer roast beef slices, cheddar cheese, green chile, and sour cream. It's warm, melty, and will surely hit the spot for a quick lunch.

INGREDIENTS;

24. ½ tbsp. diced green chilies
25. 2 tbsp. sour cream
26. 4 oz. roast beef slices
27. 2 oz. shredded Cheddar cheese

PROCEDURE;

- Tear apart the roast beef & layer it on the bottom of the dish.
- This step is important. First, spread 2 tablespoon of sour cream, followed by ½ tablespoon of the green chili.

- Layer ½ ounce of the cheddar cheese.
- One thing remains to be done now. Follow with another layer.
- Finally microwave for about 2 to 5 minutes until the cheese melts.
- Serve and Enjoy!!!

Keto Smothered Chicken

INGREDIENTS;

- 8 slices bacon, cooked & crumbled
- Salt & pepper to taste
- ½ cup barbeque sauce
- 4 boneless, skinless chicken breasts
- 1 ½ cups Cheddar cheese, shredded

PROCEDURE;

- .Then preheat oven to about 350° F. Line a baking sheet with foil & spray with non-stick spray.
- This step is important. Arrange chicken on prepared baking sheet.
- Season with salt & pepper & smother with barbeque sauce.
- Bake for about 25 to 30 minutes, or until juices run clear.
- Then remove chicken from oven.
- Top with crumbled bacon & cheese.

- One thing remains to be done now. Please Return to oven for additional for about 5 to 10 minutes to melt cheese.
- Finally alternately, melt cheese under the broiler.
- Serve and enjoy!!!!

Keto Sesame Salmon

INGREDIENTS;

- 4 salmon fillets, 4 to 6 ounce each
- 4 baby Bok Choy, trimmed & halved
- 1/2 tsp ground black pepper
- 1.5 tsp grated ginger
- 1 tbsp coconut aminos
- 1/2 lemon juice
- 1 tbsp olive oil
- 1.5 tsp sesame oil
- 2 portobello mushroom caps, about 8 ounces, sliced
- 1 tbsp toasted sesame seeds
- 1 medium-sized
- green onion, sliced
- 1/2 tsp salt

PROCEDURE;

15. Begin by preparing marinade by whisking together ginger, salt, lemon juice, black pepper, coconut aminos, sesame & olive oil.

16. Then place salmon fillet on a large bowl, drizzle with half of the prepared mari- nade & turn to coat.
17. This step is important. Cover the bowl with lid or plastic wrap & let marinate in the refrigerator for 1 hour.
18. Please in the meantime, prepare vegetables & set the oven 350°F let preheat.
19. Scatter vegetables on one side of a lined baking sheet, drizzle with remaining pre- pared marinade & toss to coat.
20. Then place marinated salmon fillets, skin-side down, on the other side of baking sheet.
21. One thing remains to be done now. Place the baking sheet into the oven & let bake for about 15 to 20 minutes or until cooked through.
22. Finally when done, remove baking sheet from the oven, sprinkle sesame seeds over salmon fillet, sprinkle with green onions & serve.

KETO DINNER

Keto Pork Chop and Broccoli Casserole

A creamy, parmesan cheese sauce gives this keto pork chop and broccoli casserole an irresistible flavor. It's a family-friendly keto meal that's easy to make and great for leftovers.

INGREDIENTS;

- 1 tbsp unsalted butter, for greasing
- 1½ lbs , ½" thick, pork chops (1 per serving)
- 1 tsp salt
- ½ tsp ground black pepper
- 1 tsp garlic crush
- 1 tsp italian spices
- 1½ tbsp olive oil, for searing
- 1 head broccoli cut into small florets
- 4 tbsp butter
- 1 cup cream cheese, sliced
- 1 cup heavy cream
- 1 cup shredded Parmesan cheese

PROCEDURE;

1. Preheat oven to 350°F. Grease a 9" x 13" baking dish with butter.
2. Pat the pork chops dry with a paper towel. Season both sides with salt, pepper, garlic powder, and Italian Spices.
3. Heat the olive oil in a large, non-stick frying pan over medium-high heat. When the oil is hot and shimmering, add the pork chops. Sear for 2 minutes per side, or until golden brown, with pink centers.
4. Put the pork chops in the baking dish, and surround them with the broccoli. Set aside.
5. Melt the butter in a saucepan, over medium heat. Stir in the heavy cream, and then add the cream cheese. Continue stirring for a couple of minutes, until smooth. Add the parmesan cheese, stirring for 2 -3 minutes more, until it becomes a creamy sauce.
6. Spread the cheese sauce over the broccoli and pork chops. Cover with aluminum foil, and bake on the middle rack for 8-10 minutes. Uncover, and

bake for another 10 minutes, or until the internal pork chop temperature is 135°F, and the edges of the cheese sauce are golden. Rest for 5 minutes, before serving.

Rotisserie Chicken with Keto Chili Béarnaise Sauce

Dressed up a simple rotisserie chicken with an amazing Keto béarnaise sauce. And the best part? It comes together in a snap. Your taste buds have been waiting for this!

INGREDIENTS;

- 3 lbs whole chicken
- 1½ cups leafy greens

Chili Béarnaise sauce

- 4 egg yolks
- 2 tsp white wine vinegar
- ½ tsp finely chopped onion
- 1 red chili pepper, deseeded and finely chopped
- 2 tsp tomato paste
- 4 tbsp butter
- salt and pepper

PROCEDURE;

1. Split the chicken into two halves and make a fresh green salad or another side dish.
2. Crack the eggs and separate the egg yolks into a heat-resistant bowl. Save the egg whites for something else.
3. Mix white-wine vinegar, chopped onion and chili in a mug. Melt the butter in a saucepan.
4. Slowly beat in the butter one drop at a time into the egg yolks and continue to whisk, increase the pace into a thin stream as the sauce thickens. Continue to whisk until all the butter has been added. The white milk protein that has accumulated at the bottom of the pan should not be included.
5. Add the vinegar and tomato paste. Stir together, salt and pepper to taste. Keep the sauce warm in a double boiler.
6. Serve with fried chicken and a green salad or another side dish of your choice.

Easy Shrimp Avocado Salad with Tomatoes

Fresh, easy, and filling! Here's a healthy and delicious shrimp avocado salad recipe for two that tastes crazy good and is also paleo, Whole30, low-carb, and gluten-free.

This shrimp avocado salad could easily be served all on its own because it really does make a complete meal. But sometimes a little extra something is nice to enjoy on the side. A few suggestions to consider are garlic keto bread a light soup or gazpacho, or low carb cheese crackers.

Loaded with the freshest ingredients.This shrimp avocado salad is a crazy healthy dinner!

INGREDIENTS;

- 225grams raw shrimp, peeled and deveined
- 1 avocado, diced

- 1 handful cherry tomatoes, diced
- 1 shallot minced
- Freshly chopped cilantro (or parsley)
- 2 tbsp butter, melted
- 1 tbsp lime juice
- 1 tbsp olove oil
- Salt and fresh cracked pepper

PROCEDURE;

1. Toss shrimp with melted butter in a bowl until well-coated.
2. Heat a skillet over medium-high heat. Add shrimp to the skillet in a single layer, searing for a minute or until it starts to become pink around the edges, then flip and cook until shrimp are cooked through, less than a minute.
3. Transfer shrimp to a shallow plate and allow to cool while you prepare the other ingredients.
4. Add all other ingredients (avocado, tomato, red onion, and cilantro) to a large mixing bowl. drizzle

with olive oil and lime juice and toss to mix everything together.
5. Add cooked shrimp and give a quick stir to mix together. Season the shrimp avocado salad with more salt and pepper, to taste. Enjoy!

Healthy, tasty, simple and quick to cook, this cod fish and asparagus skillet recipe will have you enjoy a delicious and nutritious dinner. Cod fish fillets are pan-seared to flaky perfection and tossed in a delicious lemon garlic butter sauce with asparagus. This is one seriously good fish dinner idea. Whip up this quick and delicious fish recipe tonight!

INGREDIENTS;

- 1 medium cod fillet, cut in 3 or 4 chunks (or halibut fillet)
- 1 bunches of asparagus, rinsed and trimmed
- 1 tbsp olive oil
- 1 tbsp minced garlic
- 1/2 cup white wine or vegetable broth
- 1/2 stick butter
- 1 tbsp hot sauce, optional (we used Sriracha)
- Juice of 1/2 lemon
- 1 tbsp finely chopped (or cilantro)
- chili flakes optional
- Slices of lemon, for garnish

PROCEDURE;

1. To make the garlic butter cod with lemon asparagus skillet: Season codfish with salt and pepper. set aside
2. Wash and trim the ends of the asparagus, then blanch them in boiling water for 2- 3 minutes then soak in ice water to stop cooking. This way they will cook faster and evenly in the skillet. You can skip this step if you have very thin asparagus. Drain and set aside.
3. Heat olive oil in a large skillet over medium-low heat. Gently cook fish on both sides until golden brown. Remove the cod fillets from the skillet and set aside to a plate.
4. In the same skillet over medium heat, add minced garlic then deglaze with vegetable broth (or wine). Bring it to a simmer. Add butter, lemon juice, hot sauce, and parsley. Give a quick stir to combine the lemon garlic butter sauce.
5. Add the drained blanched asparagus and toss for 2 minutes to cook it up. Add codfish fillets back to the pan and reheat for another minute. Garnish with more parsley, chili flakes, and lemon slices and serve the

garlic butter cod and lemon asparagus immediately. Enjoy!

Keto Crispy Bacon with Onion Sauce

This crispy pan-fried bacon tastes like a unique delicacy with none of the effort! Elevate the flavors with a creamy onion sauce and freshly boiled cauliflower. Enjoy this quick and tasty keto dinner any day of the week!

INGREDIENTS;

- 1 white onion finely sliced
- 1 tbsp butter
- salt and pepper
- ¾ cup heavy cream
- ½ tbsp Dijon mustard
- ½ tbsp tamari soy sauce
- 1½ lbs thick bacon or pork belly
- 400 grams cauliflower

PROCEDURE;

1. Fry the finely sliced onion in butter over medium-high heat until golden. Salt and pepper to taste.

2. Pour in the cream and bring to a boil. Stir in mustard and soy sauce.
3. Fry the bacon in a hot, dry frying pan until crispy.
4. Cut the cauliflower into small florets and cook in lightly salted water for about 10 minutes.
5. Serve the crispy pork with the onion sauce and freshly boiled cauliflower and enjoy.

Asparagus Soup

INGREDIENTS;
- 2 tbsp unsalted butter
- 1 clove garlic, minced
- 1 tbsp red onion, minced
- 1/4 tsp sea salt
- 1/8 tsp black pepper
- 1-1/2 cup asparagus chopped into 1-1/2" pieces
- 3 cups vegetable stock
- 1/3 cup heavy cream

PROCEDURE;
- Combine butter, onion, and garlic in a medium saucepan.
- Add asparagus to the pan and continue to sauté 4 more minutes.
- Remove the tips of the asparagus from the pan and set aside.
- Add the vegetable stock, salt, and pepper to the pan and simmer for another 6 minutes.
- Use a hand immersion stick blender to blend the soup until smooth.
- Return add the asparagus tips and the cream into

soup.
- Once the soup is heated through, divide it evenly into four bowls.then the lemon juice evenly over the asparagus.
- Sprinkle salt, pepper, and zest over the top of the asparagus.
- Place in the oven for about 15 minutes until desired tenderness is achieved.
- Sprinkle parmesan over the asparagus as soon as it is removed from the oven.
- Divide evenly between two plates. Sauté butter, onions, and garlic in a medium skillet over medium-low heat until onions are translucent.
- Add the heavy cream, pepper, salt, dill, and zest. Simmer uncovered for 3-4 minutes, and then remove from heat.
- Slightly cool and add the Greek yogurt. Place one salmon filet on each plate and divide sauce equally be- tween them.

Swedish Meatballs

INGREDIENTS;
5. 4 tbsp butter
6. 1 medium, onion, chopped
7. 1 lb. ground beef
8. 1/4 cup crushed pork rinds
9. 1/2 tsp salt
10. 1/2 tsp ground black pepper
11. 1/4 tsp allspice
12. 1/4 tsp nutmeg
13. 1/4 tsp garlic powder
14. 1 egg
15. 1 tsp Dijon mustard
16. 3/4 tsp arrowroot powder
17. 2 tbsp cold water
18. 1 cup beef broth
19. 1/2 cup heavy cream
20. 16 ounces Tofu and Shirataki noodles

PROCEDURE;
23. Melt a tablespoon of butter in large skillet and sauté onion in it over medium heat.
24. Combine beef, pork rind, beaten egg, onion, salt, spices, and 2 tablespoons heavy cream in a

large bowl.
25. Combine thoroughly. Divide into 16 equal sized meatballs. Melt the rest of the butter in the skillet over medium heat and add the meatballs.
26. Cook until meatballs are cooked through, moving them so they brown on all sides as they cook, about 15 minutes.
27. Remove from heat and transfer to a plate. Add the broth, remaining cream, and mustard to the pan and simmer on low, scraping the bottom for flavor.
28. Mix the arrowroot powder and water in a small mea- suring cup to make a slurry and add it to the sauce. Continue simmering on low until the sauce is the desired thickness.
29. Return the meatballs to the sauce and simmer a couple minutes longer. Cover and remove from heat. Prepare noodles according to package directions, draining well.
30. Evenly divide the noodles between four plates.
31. Then cover each bed of noodles with an equal amount of sauce and four meatballs.

BBQ Chicken Wings with Loaded Mash Cauliflower

INGREDIENTS;

BBQ Chicken Rub:

4. 2 tsp garlic powder
5. 2 tsp onion powder
6. 2 tsp gourmet smoked paprika
7. 1 tbsp Xylitol or equivalent measurement of the zero carb sweetener.
8. 1 tsp cayenne pepper
9. 1/2 tsp ground ginger
10. 1/2 tsp cumin
11. 1/2 tsp cinnamon
12. 1/2 tsp coriander
13. 1/4 tsp salt
14. 1/4 tsp black pepper

BBQ Chicken:

- 2 pounds skin-on, chicken wings
- 2 tsp coconut oil
- 3 tsp tomato puree
- 1 tbsp coconut oil

- 1/2 cup chicken stock
- 1 tbsp butter
- 1 tsp mustard

Loaded Cauliflower Mash:

- 1 pound cauliflower
- 1 tbsp butter
- 1/2 cup sour cream
- 1 clove garlic, minced
- 1/8 tsp salt
- 1/4 tsp black pepper
- 2 slices bacon, cooked, and chopped into small pieces
- 1/2 cup cheddar cheese, shredded
- 1 tbsp chives, chopped

PROCEDURE;

1. Preheat oven to F.350°F
2. Make rub by combining all the ingredients for it and mixing until well-blended.
3. Place half (about 6 teaspoons) into a small saucepan.
4. Grease a baking dish with 2 teaspoons coconut

oil, using all of it.

5. Arrange wings in the dish in a single layer and sprinkle remaining rub on top, rubbing it into the meat.

6. Bake wings in oven for 40 minutes. Steam the cauliflower using the microwave by placing it in a microwave safe bowl with three tablespoons of water and covering.

7. Microwave on high about 5 minutes adding 2 minutes at a time after that until cauliflower is soft and easy to break apart.

8. Immediately drain any excess water and allow to sit in colander for 5 minutes. Transfer to food processor with butter, garlic, sour cream, salt, and pepper.

9. Process until desired consistency. Transfer mash to an oven safe baking dish. Evenly sprinkle bacon and cheddar over the top.

10. When the chicken comes out of the oven, place the remaining coconut oil , but- ter, tomato puree, and mustard into the pan with the rub.

11. Over low heat, whisk the sauce together, slowly adding in the stock. Once the stock is the correct consistency, remove from heat and pour over chicken immediately.

12. Place mash in oven and return chicken and sauce to the oven for another 20-25 minutes.
13. Divide chicken wings onto four plates with about 1/2 pound of wings on each and divide the mash evenly between the plates

Pot Roast

INGREDIENTS;

- 48 ounces boneless, lean chuck roast
- 2 tsp Kosher salt
- 1-1/2 tsp coconut oil
- 5 large stalks celery
- 1 cup carrots, chopped
- 1/2 cup onions, chopped
- 4 cups beef broth
- 3 tsp thyme freshly chopped
- 1/4 tsp black pepper

PROCEDURE;

1. In a stock pot over medium-high heat, melt the coconut oil.
2. Season the beef with one teaspoon of salt on each side and place it in the pan to brown for approximately 5 minutes on each side.
3. Add all the other ingredients to the pot and simmer, covered, on low heat for approximately 2 hours until meat is cooked to desired doneness.

4. Evenly divide the vegetables and meat between six plates.

Garlic-Rosemary Pork Chops with Roasted Brussels Sprouts

INGREDIENTS;

Pork Chops:
- 2 lb bone-in pork chops, center cut (ideally would be 4 chops)
- 1-1/2 tsp Kosher salt
- 1/2 tsp black pepper
- 4 tbsp fresh rosemary, broken into 2 sprigs
- 4 cloves garlic, whole
- 4 tbsp salted butter
- 2-1/2 tbsp apple cider vinegar
- 1-1/2 tbsp ghee (clarified butter)

Brussels Sprouts:
7. 12-1/2 ounces Brussels sprouts
8. 4 slices bacon, raw, chopped
9. 2 tbsp capers
10. 1 tbsp olive oil
11. 1/8 tsp sea salt
12. 1/8 tsp black pepper

PROCEDURE;

- Preheat the oven to 350°F.
- Slice Brussels sprouts in half and arrange in a single layer in a baking dish.
- Toss with bacon, olive oil, salt, and pepper. Bake 15 minutes.
- Sprinkle the pork chops with the salt and pepper on both sides.
- Melt the ghee in a large skillet on low, then add the pork chops. Sear 5-7 minutes on each side be- fore flipping.
- After you flip, add butter, rosemary, and garlic to the skillet. As the butter melts, spoon it over the chops.
- Remove the chops and add the vinegar to the skillet. Scrape the pan as you mix the vinegar, seasoning, and butter. Remove Brussels sprouts from oven.
- Add capers and toss again.
- Return to oven for another 5-8 minutes until bacon is crisp.
- Divide into 4 equal portions and place on plates with chops.
- Drizzle butter mix- ture from pan over each chop.

Chicken Cordon Bleu with Garlic Keto Bread

INGREDIENTS;

Chicken Cordon Bleu:
- 24 ounces boneless, skinless chicken breast
- 1/2 tsp salt
- 1/2 tsp black pepper
- 4 slices deli ham
- 4-1/2 ounces Swiss cheese, sliced
- 12 slices bacon, raw
- 4 tsp olive oil
- 1/2 cup shredded parmesan
- 2 tbsp parsley

Bread:
5. 1 cup almond flour
6. 1 tsp double-acting baking powder
7. 1/8 tsp Kosher salt
8. 1/4 tsp xanthan gum
9. 1/2 cup butter
10. 2 tbsp coconut oil

11.   6 eggs, separated

Garlic Butter:
- 1clove garlic, minced
- 1/4 cup finely grated (fresh) Parmesan cheese
- 4 tbsp butter

PROCEDURE;
1. Preheat oven to 375° F.
2. Begin by whipping together the garlic, parmesan cheese, and butter to make the garlic butter. Set aside to keep it soft and at room temperature.
3. In a food processor, combine the dry parts of the bread recipe flour, baking powder, salt, and xanthan gum as well as the fats: butter and coconut oil.
4. When a dough forms, add in the egg yolks. Blend the egg whites until they reach a soft peak stage.
5. Carefully fold these into the batter and then pour into a parchment lined loaf pan that is greased on the sides with butter. Bake 25- 30 minutes and allow to cool completely.
6. Butterfly chicken breasts and pound to 1/2-inch thickness using a meat tender- izer.
7. Sprinkle salt and pepper evenly over inside portion of the chicken. Place one slice of ham on

each chicken breast and arrange Swiss cheese in a single layer over ham.
8. Fold the chicken to return it to its original form, being careful to keep the ham and cheese on the inside of the fold.
9. Wrap each breast in bacon, using 3 slices to evenly wrap each. Keep the ends of the bacon underneath the chicken to prevent it from unwrapping.
10. Heat olive oil in a large skillet on medium high heat. Add wrapped chicken and cover. Cook chicken for about 5 minutes on each side or until the chicken is cooked through and juices are clear.
11. Sprinkle with parmesan cheese and cover again until the cheese melts, about 45 seconds.
12. Preheat the broiler. Slice the cooled bread in half length-wise and then slice each half in half again parallel to the counter.
13. Butter the bread with one-fourth of the garlic butter and place face up on a baking pan. Broil 2 minutes until butter and cheese have melted.

BEEF CHILI

PROCEDURE;
- 2-1/2 pounds ground beef
- 1/2 large white onion
- 4 cloves garlic, minced
- 30 ounces canned, diced tomatoes with liquid
- 6 ounces canned tomato paste
- 4 ounces canned green chilies with liquid
- 1/4 cup chili powder
- 2 tbsp Worcestershire sauce
- 2 tbsp cumin
- 1 tbsp dried oregano
- 2 tsp sea salt
- 1 tsp black peppe

PROCEDURE;
- Cook the onion, garlic, and ground beef in a large skillet over medium-high heat for about 15 minutes until the onions are translucent and the beef is browned, stirring to break beef into small pieces.
- Place beef in a slow cooker and add the remaining

ingredients. Mix well.
- Set the slow cooker to low and cook 6-8 hours or to high and cook 3-4 hours.

Keto Stuffed Mushrooms

INGREDIENTS;

21. 1 ½ lbs Baby Bella mushrooms, stems removed
22. ¼ Cup Mayonnaise
23. 1 tsp oregano, dried
24. 3 ½ tbsp Chives, finely chopped
25. 1 lb Blue Crab Meat, finely shredded
26. ½ tsp Paprika

PROCEURE;

1. Combine the shredded crab with the mayonnaise, the chives & the spices in a large bowl
2. This step is important. Set the mixture aside for about 15 to 20 minutes; then pre- heat the oven to about 350° F.
3. Now clean the Bella mushrooms & make sure to remove the stems; then pat it dry with clean paper towels

4. Stuff the mushroom caps with the shredded crab mixture; then place it over a baking sheet lined with a large parchment paper.
5. Then bake the stuffed mushrooms for about 15 to 20 minutes.
6. One thing remains to be done now. Remove the stuffed mushrooms from the oven & let rest for about 2 minutes.
7. Finally serve & enjoy your stuffed mushrooms!

Crazy Grilled Eggplant Panini

INGREDIENTS;

- 8 basil leaves, chopped
- 1.5 tsp minced garlic
- 2 tbsp pine nuts, toasted
- 2.5 tbsp mayonnaise, organic
- 1 cup baby spinach
- 2 small tomatoes
- 2 small Eggplants, destemmed
- ½ cup shredded mozzarella cheese

PROCEDURE;

- Switch on countertop grill, set at medium heat setting & let preheat.
- Place a medium-sized skillet pan over medium heat, grease with oil & when heat- ed, add garlic.
- This step is important. Let cook for about 2 to 5 minutes or until nicely golden brown or fragrant.
- When done, remove the pan from heat & let cool.
- In the meantime, cut each eggplant in half.

- Now prepare aioli by placing mayonnaise in a bowl & then add cooled garlic & basil.
- Stir until well combined & then spread this mixture onto slices of eggplants.
- Please layer two slices evenly with spinach, cheese, tomato slices, & nuts.
- Cover with other eggplant slices, aioli side down & place onto heated grill.
- One thing remains to be done now. Close with its lid & let grill until cheese melt completely.
- Finally serve immediately and enjoy!!!

Crab-stuffed Mushrooms with Cream Cheese

INGREDIENTS;
- 14. 20 oz. baby Bella mushrooms (20-25)
- 15. 2 tbsp. grated parmesan cheese
- 16. 1.5 tbsp. freshly chopped parsley
- 17. Salt

Ingredients for the Filling:
- 4 oz. of each Finely chopped crab meat
- Cream cheese
- 1 t. dried oregano
- ½ t. of each Black pepper
- Paprika
- 5 minced cloves of garlic
- ¼ t. of salt

PROCEDURE;

5. Warm up the oven to about 380ºF. Line a baking tin with parchment paper.
6. This step is important. Do the Prep: Discard the stems from the mushrooms.

7. Now mince the garlic & finely chop the crab meat.
8. Arrange the mushroom caps on the baking tin about one inch apart. Sprinkle them with the salt.
9. One thing remains to be done now. Combine the filling components & mix until smooth.

Finally stuff the caps & bake for about 25 to 30 minutes in the prepared oven.

Coconut Pork Butt Curry

INGREDIENTS;

- 32 oz Pork Butt (Diced)
- 8 oz Green Beans
- 1.5 tsp Grounded Coriander
- 1 Tsp Grounded Cumin
- ½ tsp Grounded Cinnamon
- ½ tsp Chili Powder
- 1 Shallots Diced
- 3 Cloves minced
- 1 inch Ginger Sliced
- 1 Lime Juice
- 14 oz Coconut Cream
- 2 tbsp Coconut Oil
- ½ tsp Salt

PROCEDURE;

1. Add Pork, Coriander, Cumin, Cinnamon, & Chili Powder in a bowl & mix well. Marinate them in plastic bag for about 25 to 30 minutes.

2. This step is important. heat up a pan to medium heat with Coconut Oil. Add Onion, Ginger, & Onion to the pan & sauté for about 2 to 5 minutes.
3. Please cook the Pork in the pan for about 5 to 10 minutes for about 5 to 10 min- utes until it turns brown.
4. Then add Coconut Cream & let it simmer for about 75 to 80 minutes until pork is tender.
5. One thing remains to be done now. Add Green Beans, Lime Juice Salt & cook for about 2 to 5 more minutes.
6. Finally Serve & enjoy!

Easy Bacon Prapped Pork Tenderloin

INGREDIENTS;

- 2.5 tbsp of soy sauce
- 1 lb of pork tenderloin, excess fat removed
- 4 slices of bacon
- 1 tsp of garlic paste
- 1 tsp onion powder
- 2.5 tbsp of dry white wine

PROCEDURE;

- Place the tenderloin in a big plastic bag & add the garlic paste, onion, powder, whine & soy sauce. Shake well & let marinate on the fridge for at least 3 to 4 hours before cooking.
- This step is important. Transfer the marinated tenderloin onto a cutting board & reserve the marinade aside.
- Line the 4 pieces of bacon next to each other, place the tenderloin on one of the edges & wrap the bacon around it.
- Bake in a preheated oven 380°F for 30 minutes.

- Warm up the marinade in a small pan, add a few drizzles of extra wine or water & once it has started to bubble remove from the heat.
- One thing remains to be done now. Pour over the cooked tenderloin
- Finally serve ideally with arugula salad.

Bacon Net Pork Tenderloin

INGREDIENTS;

12. 17.6 oz Pork Tenderloin
13. 14.1 oz Gluten-free Sausage Meat
14. 16 Thin Slices Bacon
15. 1 White onion Finely chopped
16. 2 Cloves Garlic minced
17. 1.5 Tsp Dried Thyme
18. ¼ Cup Flax meal
19. 1.5 Tbsp Butter
20. Salt & Pepper to taste

PROCEDURE;

- Heat up a pan to medium-high heat with Butter.
- Add in Onion & Garlic & stir for few minutes.

- This step is important. Add in Sausage Meat & break into small pieces. Fry for 6-8 minutes until they all turn brown, & then transfer them to a bowl.
- Add Flax meal, Salt & Pepper to the same bowl. Reserve aside.
- Preheat oven to 350 °F.
- Now Slice the Tenderloin in half with 1 cm meat remain connecting.
- Open it like a book & cover it with a piece of cling film.
- Then pound it with a meat tenderizer until about 1 cm thin. Set it aside when it is done.
- Lay 8 Bacons on chopping board & place 8 Bacons in alternating order to form a net.
- Place the Tenderloin on top of the net. Place Sausage filling on top & roll up the Tenderloin.
- Please roll up the net carefully with Tenderloin & fillings inside.
- Fix the ends with toothpicks to secure all fillings inside.
- Now bake the roll over baking sheet for about 40 to 45 minutes until ther- mometer reach 150 °F & Bacon turns crispy.

- One thing remains to be done now. Remove it from oven & rest for about 5 to 10 minutes. Remove toothpick & slice into portions.
- Finally serve & enjoy!

Sausage, Shrimp and Zucchini Skewers

INGREDIENTS;

14. 3 large smoked sausages cut into 30-35 slices in total
15. 1 packet of low carb barbeque sauce
16. 2 medium-sized zucchinis, cut into 35-40 slices
17. 40 shrimps, peeled with tail on

PROCEDURE;

- Take 20 medium skewers & soak in water first so they don't get burned while cooking.
- This step is important. Take each skewer & thread 2 pieces of shrimp, two of zucchini & two of sausages (one ingredient, then another to make a pattern).
- One thing remains to be done now. Brush the barbeque sauce over the shrimp & zucchini & cook over a grill pan for about 2 to 5 minutes on each side.

- Finally serve optionally with chopped lettuce & some extra barbeque sauce. Something is special!!
- Serve and enjoy!!!

keto snacks and sweets

JALAPENO POPPER BALLS

INGREDIENTS;

- 3 oz. of cream cheese
- 3 slices of bacon
- 1 jalapeno pepper
- 1/2 tsp dried parsley
- 1/4 tsp onion powder
- 1/4 tsp garlic powder
- salt and pepper, to taste

PROCEDURE;

1. Place a medium-sized skillet over medium heat.
2. Fry the bacon until very crispy. Once cooled, crumble.

3. Remove the bacon and set onto one side. Keep the leftover grease for later use.
4. Slice and de-seed the jalapeno pepper. Now, finely dice.
5. In a mixing bowl, add the jalapeno and spices with the cream cheese and season with salt and pepper. Mix until well combined.
6. Add the leftover bacon fat and mix until a solid ball has formed.
7. Crumble the crispy bacon onto a plate.
8. Divide the cream cheese mixture into 3 or 4 and then roll into balls with clean hands.
9. Now roll the balls in the bacon bits to cover well.

HONEY-KETO MUFFINS

INGREDIENTS;

8. 1/2 a cup of blanched almond flour
9. 1/2 a cup of flaxseed meal
10. 1 tbsp psyllium husk powder
11. 1/4 tsp salt
12. 1/4 tsp baking powder
13. 3 tbsp organic honey
14. 1/4 of a cup of butter, melted
15. 1 egg
16. 1/3 cup sour cream
17. 1/4 of a cup of coconut milk
18. 3 hot dogs

PROCEDURE;

- Preheat oven to 250°F
- In a large mixing bowl, mix the dry ingredients well.

- Add in the egg, butter, sour cream, and then mix well until combined.
- When everything is incorporated, add the coconut milk and continue
  mixing until you have a thick batter.
- Divide the batter between 20 greased muffin holes.
- Cut the hot dogs into 20 pieces and push a piece into each muffin
  hole.
- Bake for around 12 minutes. Put under the broiler for 1 to 3 minutes,
  or until the tops brown a little.

KETO MICROWAVED BROWNIES

INGREDIENT;

18. 1 tbsp unsalted butter
19. 1 (beaten) egg white
20. 1 tsp cocoa powder, unsweetened
21. 1/8 tspvanilla extract
22. 3 drops of liquid stevia
23. 1 pinch of baking soda
24. 1 pinch of salt

PROCEDURE;

- Find a microwave-safe mug or container.
- In a small bowl, add the egg white and beat until they are aerated (nice and frothy).
- Place all ingredients in the mug and mix well with a fork.
- Microwave for about 40 seconds. You might have to experiment.
- Not all microwaves are equal in power setting functionality.
- For a "molten" consistency, knock off 10 seconds.

- Remove from microwave and top with maple syrup or cocoa powder.

CHOCOLATE AD COCONUT CHEESECAKE

INGREDIENTS;

Base
- 1/4 cup almond meal
- 1/3 cup shredded coconut,
- 1-2 tbsp of honey, to taste
- 2 tbsp melted butter

Filling
10. 1 cup of cream cheese
11. 6 tbsp coconut cream
12. 2 tbsp cocoa powder
13. 2 tablespoons of honey
14. 2 teaspoons of coconut essence

PROCEDURE;

Base
- Preheat oven to 180°F and lightly grease eight holes of a standard sized muffin tin (you can use non-stick spray if you wish).

- In a mixing bowl, add the almond meal, coconut, honey and the meltedbutter.
- •Using clean hands, mix well until everything becomes combined.
- •Divide the mixture into 8 portions and press into the muffin tin holes.
- •Bake for 10 minutes, or until they turn golden brown.Remove from oven and let cool.

Filling

7. In a mixing bowl, add all the ingredients for the filling.
8. Using a hand mixer mix on low speed, blend until everything has combined.
9. Once combined, increase speed to medium-high for 3 minutes.
10. Spoon the mixture evenly between the cooled bases.
11. Place in the refrigerator (before serving) for one hour.

CRISPY-BAKED PARSNIP CHIPS

INGREDIENTS;

- 2 medium parsnips, peeled and thinly sliced
- olive oil, for coating
- salt to taste

PROCEDURE;

- Preheat oven to 180°F
- In a bowl, add the parsnip chips and drizzle with olive oil.
- Mix withclean hands and cover every side of the parsnip chips.
- Place on a lined baking sheet and leave space in-between chips.
- Bake for around 6 to 8 minutes, or until turning golden brown.
- Remove from oven and sprinkle with salt. Let cool before eating.

CRISPY-BAKED KALE CHIPS

INGREDIENTS;

- kale leaves
- olive oil
- seasonings of choice

PROCEDURE;

1. Preheat the oven to 250°F
2. Wash and pat dry the kale leaves, thoroughly.
3. Tear leaves into medium-sized pieces.
4. Add to a large mixing bowl, a small amount of olive oil.
5. Add kale leaves and spices.
6. Mix with clean hands to coat all sides of the leaves.
7. Place on baking sheet. Leave space in-between so air can pass through.
8. Bake until crispy for around 8 to 10 minutes. Check at 2-minute intervals.

KETO ENERGY-BOOSTING PROTEIN SHAKE

INGREDIENTS;

- 1 and a 1/2 cup of almond milk
- 1 tbsp coconut oil
- 1 tbsp peanut butter
- 1 scoop of vanilla (or chocolate) protein powder
- 4 or 5 ice cubes

PROCEDURE;

- Add all the ingredients into a blender.
- Blend on high until you have a thick, creamy consistency.
- Pour and drink immediately, while cool.

www.ingramcontent.com/pod-product-compliance
Lightning Source LLC
Chambersburg PA
CBHW070859080526
44589CB00013B/1130